# NEW ENGLAND LIGHTHOUSES

## A BOOK OF 21 POSTCARDS

W9-DCG-571

BROWNTROUT PUBLISHERS
SAN FRANCISCO • CALIFORNIA

# BROWNTROUT PUBLISHERS

P. O. BOX 280070
SAN FRANCISCO • CALIFORNIA 94128-0070
800 777 7812


ISBN: 1-56313-930-8
TITLE: 930

BROWNTROUT publishes a large line of calendars, photographic books, and postcard books.
*Please write for more information.*

Printed in Korea

# NEW ENGLAND LIGHTHOUSES
Sunset over Bass Head Light, Mt. Desert Island, Maine

BROWNTROUT PUBLISHERS • SAN FRANCISCO, CALIFORNIA

# NEW ENGLAND LIGHTHOUSES
Point Judith Light with rising full moon, Point Judith, Rhode Island

PUBLISHED BY BROWNTROUT • SAN FRANCISCO, CALIFORNIA

# NEW ENGLAND LIGHTHOUSES
Wood End Light, Cape Cod National Seashore, Massachusetts

PUBLISHED BY BROWNTROUT • SAN FRANCISCO, CALIFORNIA

# NEW ENGLAND LIGHTHOUSES
Prospect Harbor Light, Prospect Harbor, Maine

PUBLISHED BY BROWNTROUT • SAN FRANCISCO, CALIFORNIA

# NEW ENGLAND LIGHTHOUSES
Cape Poge Light, Martha's Vineyard, Massachusetts

PUBLISHED BY BROWNTROUT • SAN FRANCISCO, CALIFORNIA

# NEW ENGLAND LIGHTHOUSES
Nobska Light, Cape Cod, Massachusetts

PUBLISHED BY BROWNTROUT • SAN FRANCISCO, CALIFORNIA

# NEW ENGLAND LIGHTHOUSES
Portland Head Light, Maine

PUBLISHED BY BROWNTROUT • SAN FRANCISCO, CALIFORNIA

# NEW ENGLAND LIGHTHOUSES
Cape Neddick Light, also known as Nubble Light, York, Maine

PUBLISHED BY BROWNTROUT • SAN FRANCISCO, CALIFORNIA

# NEW ENGLAND LIGHTHOUSES
Sunrise on West Quoddy Head Light, Lubec, Maine

PUBLISHED BY BROWNTROUT • SAN FRANCISCO, CALIFORNIA

# NEW ENGLAND LIGHTHOUSES
Hendricks Head Light, Boothbay Harbor, Maine

PUBLISHED BY BROWNTROUT • SAN FRANCISCO, CALIFORNIA

# NEW ENGLAND LIGHTHOUSES
Stage Harbor Light, Chatham, Massachusetts

PUBLISHED BY BROWNTROUT • SAN FRANCISCO, CALIFORNIA

# NEW ENGLAND LIGHTHOUSES
Evening sky at Pemaquid Point Lighthouse, Bristol, Maine

PUBLISHED BY BROWNTROUT • SAN FRANCISCO, CALIFORNIA

# NEW ENGLAND LIGHTHOUSES
Brant Point Light, Nantucket Island, Massachusetts

PUBLISHED BY BROWNTROUT • SAN FRANCISCO, CALIFORNIA

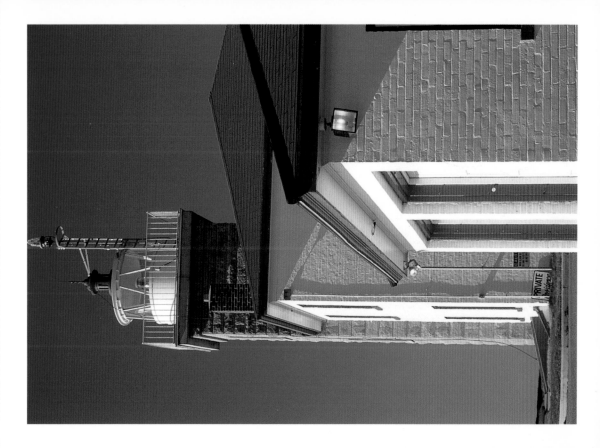

# NEW ENGLAND LIGHTHOUSES
Watch Hill Light, Watch Hill, Rhode Island

PUBLISHED BY BROWNTROUT • SAN FRANCISCO, CALIFORNIA

# NEW ENGLAND LIGHTHOUSES
Owl's Head Light, Rockland, Maine

PUBLISHED BY BROWNTROUT • SAN FRANCISCO, CALIFORNIA

# NEW ENGLAND LIGHTHOUSES
North Light at Sandy Point, Block Island, Rhode Island

PUBLISHED BY BROWNTROUT • SAN FRANCISCO, CALIFORNIA

# NEW ENGLAND LIGHTHOUSES
Fort Constitution Lighthouse, New Castle, New Hampshire

PUBLISHED BY BROWNTROUT • SAN FRANCISCO, CALIFORNIA

# NEW ENGLAND LIGHTHOUSES
Stage Harbor Lighthouse, Chatham, Massachusetts

PUBLISHED BY BROWNTROUT • SAN FRANCISCO, CALIFORNIA

# NEW ENGLAND LIGHTHOUSES
Rockland Breakwater Light, Rockland, Maine

PUBLISHED BY BROWNTROUT • SAN FRANCISCO, CALIFORNIA

# NEW ENGLAND LIGHTHOUSES
Marshall Point Light, Port Clyde, Maine

PUBLISHED BY BROWNTROUT • SAN FRANCISCO, CALIFORNIA

# NEW ENGLAND LIGHTHOUSES
Nauset Light, Cape Cod National Seashore, Massachusetts

PUBLISHED BY BROWNTROUT • SAN FRANCISCO, CALIFORNIA